MIRELLE SIMON
WORK FROM HOME

The Ultimate Guide on How to Find Legitimate Work From Home Jobs, Learn the Foolproof Methods on How to Find Work and Earn Money Online

Descrierea CIP a Bibliotecii Naționale a României
MIRELLE SIMON
   WORK FROM HOME. The Ultimate Guide on How to
Find Legitimate Work From Home Jobs, Learn the Foolproof
Methods on How to Find Work and Earn Money Online /
Mirelle Simon – Bucharest: Editura My Ebook, 2021
   ISBN

MIRELLE SIMON

WORK FROM HOME

The Ultimate Guide on How to Find Legitimate Work From Home Jobs, Learn the Foolproof Methods on How to Find Work and Earn Money Online

My Ebook Publishing House
Bucharest, 2021

TABLE OF CONTENTS

Introduction 7

CHAPTER 1: **Defining Your Skillset** 11

CHAPTER 2: **Work At Home Options** 13

CHAPTER 3: **Finding Clients & Getting Hired** 21

CHAPTER 4: **Tips To Getting Started** 24

CHAPTER 5: **Finding Online Work** 34

INTRODUCTION

Are you interested in making money online? Love the idea of working from the comfort of your own home, setting your own schedule and being your own boss?

In order to be successful working from home however, you need to *fully commit* to the process of securing and completing home based assignments and projects.

If you approach your work at home job search as a spare time hobby, instead of handling it with professionalism like you would an in-house position or a regular full time job, it's unlikely that you are going to be dedicated enough to stick to the process, much less be consistently successful with the positions that you accept.

To be honest, working at home is very rewarding yet extremely challenging. You are responsible for completing tasks, staying on schedule and making sure that you fufill client requests and obligations on time.

With no supervisor or boss looking over your shoulder, being a successful telecommuter requires strict discipline and dedication.

Another important element to becoming a successful freelancer is in being able to *quickly adapt to changes in the industry*.

You need to be able to instantly shift gears and change your format in order to stay competitive (if you are creating your own client lists) or to be able to cater to your online employers need for reoccuring change in direction.

The methods that we use to complete our projects, the format that we use as a foundation, and even the methods of communicating with our clients or employers is constantly changing, and in order to remain in demand, you will need to be able to keep the pace, and modify your business plan whenever required.

Throughout the years, I've experienced incredible highs and dramatic lows. There were times when I couldn't keep up with client projects and other times where I was struggling to find enough work to maintain my business.

When it comes to freelancing, stability doesn't always come with the territory, and so by creating a solid action plan that will enable you to consistently make money, and by always focusing on staying competitive and growing your business, you will be able to get through any temporary downtimes that you may encounter (and we all experience this at one time or another).

As a **telecommuter**, you are typically considered a work at home **employee** for a company or online business. This means, that you are often required to follow specific schedules and meet pre-determined deadlines.

Quite often, the company that you work for covers a portion of your operational costs such as Internet connection or office equipment.

As a **freelancer**, you are working for yourself, finding your own clients, setting your own schedules and developing your own business structure.

You would be responsible for all associated costs, as well as in claiming all relevant tax deductions from running your own home based business.

When it comes to work at home jobs, where you are a paid telecommuter working for companies and clients, you can generate revenue from content development, website development and creation, as well as by offering services, such as search engine optimization, marketing, and even working as a virtual assistant.

This is where people get confused, because while there are stark differences in the way that you perform your tasks as either a freelancer or telecommuter (based on structuring schedules, communicating with employers or clients, etc), the opportunities themselves, are often relatively similar, including positions in data entry, transcription work, typist, virtual secretary, marketer or researcher.

It's time to get excited about what is in store for you, because this book focuses on the top work at home opportunities and options that will help you get started in choosing the right work at home success plan that will help you reach your goals!

Regardless of your skill set, or interest, there's something just for you within the work at home arena. From high paid freelance positions, to carving out your own brand and business, you'll gain a closer look at the top opportunities online.

Let's get started!

CHAPTER 1

DEFINING YOUR SKILLSET

In order to begin setting up your business and recruiting customers and clients, you need to determine what your passions are, as well as what you can bring to the table.

There are many different work at home opportunities available to you. From writing, programming, design services, and even offline business consulting, the doors are wide open with an abundance of opportunities at your fingertips.

Begin by evaluating what skills you could turn into profit.

Do you enjoy writing content? Are you familiar with SEO? Are you proficient with installing scripts, or programming? Do you enjoy working with others in an environment where you directly help merchants and business owners get started? Or perhaps you prefer working solo, and would find greater passion in a multitude of short- term projects.

It's important to closely evaluate your skillset so you can build your services around existing knowledge and skills. You can also expand your services later on, to include other freelancers who can contribute to your projects, and who you could outsource work to while still making a profit.

In the beginning stages however, you'll need to rely on your own expertise, and even if you lack the "business know how", chances are that you have some sort of skill that would be a valuable asset to business owners, marketers and professionals.

For some people, a faster smarter better way to discover a work at home fit for themselves is to visit

http://fastersmarterbetter.com

This site helps people become entrepreneurs online by providing guidance and tools and resources.

CHAPTER 2

WORK AT HOME OPTIONS

Writing & Content Opportunities

Content powers the Internet. It's an important component to both start-up and established websites and companies. Fresh, high quality and targeted content drives in traffic, and ultimately helps business owners connect with their target audience.

If you are able to produce quality content and material, you'll quickly build a client base that will keep you in business for many years to come.

One of the most important decisions you'll make as a content provider is to determine what **"segment"** of a market you'll cater to. In other words, you want to become a "content specialist" focusing on specific services.

For example, content writers cover many different fields including:

- **Copywriting** – Writing sales copy and promotional material.

- **Information Products** – Creating ebooks, white papers & reports.

- **Instructional Writer** – Creates training material (courses, etc.)

- **Bloggers** – Create blog specific content that engage audiences and focus primarily on "conversational points".

- **Article Writers** – Specialize in "SEO", writing articles that attract both people and the search engines.

You'll want to choose one area of specialty to start with, so you can begin to build a brand around your name and service. You can then expand to include additional content-based services that appeal to a broader audience.

Programming

One of the most sought after in the freelance industry are top-notch programmers and coders.

Online businesses, entrepreneurs and marketers alike are always interested in being able to provide their customers with unique tools that automate tasks, increase productivity or simplify projects.

If you've got the skills and experience to develop interactive scripts, software, plugins and code, you can quickly carve out a name for yourself in the online business arena.

Business Consultant

If you're business savvy, and interested in working closely with start-up companies and businesses, you can make a full time income offering consulting services to offline, local businesses.

Everywhere around you, new and established businesses are looking to establish an online presence, and many of them simply don't know where to start.

You can easily build a very profitable business offering a variety of services that include:

- Web & Graphic Design
- Search Engine Optimization
- Online Marketing
- Content Development
- Social Media Management
- Website Updates & Maintenance
- Email Marketing

Better yet, you could easily branch out and expand your service list by offering hosting, and other services where you simply serve as the middleman, connecting businesses to resources they need.

Graphic Designer

If you love creating graphics and presentations, you'll want to consider offering graphic design services to online businesses.

Every business needs a website, and graphics help to develop a unique brand and presence that builds credibility and leaves an everlasting impression.

There are many different areas within the graphic design arena that you could cater to, including:

- Web Design
- Customized Blog Themes
- Digital Product Covers & Images
- Promotional Material (banners, etc)

When it comes to finding work in the graphic design industry, turn to popular freelance marketplaces including http://www.eLance.com and http://www.Guru.com but also include freelance community sites, primarily focusing on web development, including:

http://www.iFreelance.com
http://www.oDesk.com
http://www.Project4Hire.com

You can also start making money participating in design and graphic competitions and contents. Not only is this a great way to make money, but you'll be able to generate exposure and garner attention for your design services!

Social Media Consultant

With the growing popularity of social marketing, small businesses are always looking to maximize exposure by building a presence within sites like Facebook and Twitter.

Social Media Consultants and Managers create, manage and maintain social media accounts, including:

Posting regular updates Managing followers Creating Fan & Media Pages Promoting upcoming launches

You can find many different opportunities in social media through freelance marketplaces, as well as with local businesses.

http://www.LocalMarketingMaven.com will help you get started, and you can also begin accepting work by participating in open job sites and offers, including:

http://www.eLance.com (see "Social Media Marketing Jobs")

http://www.Indeed.com

http://www.Guru.com http://www.SimplyHired.com

Virtual Assistant

Virtual assistants are a necessity for large businesses outsourcing work who need extra 'hands on deck' to complete daily tasks and projects.

For the most part, virtual assistants are responsible for handling telephone calls relating to the company, setting up appointments, handling projects, managing task lists and quite often, are even responsible for website maintenance .

If you are thinking about getting into virtual assistant work keep in mind that the more skills and experience that you have the better your chances will be of getting a good job. You may want to take a course or work to receive certification in relevant fields to increase your qualifications and chances of landing the highest paying opportunities.

As a virtual assistant you'll need to be comfortable completing various clerical and administrative tasks without constant supervision.

Producing excellent work results will keep clients coming your way. A consistent flow of clients allows you to grow your work from home business and create some stability.

There are necessary tools to make your virtual assistant career excel. A stable highspeed Internet connection, reliable computer, quiet office space, standard phone line, and an all in one printer will provide you with a good start for this work from home business.

Being able to organized work tasks is another major component to the success of your virtual assistance career. Depending on the clients you choose to work with, there may be tons of tasks for you to complete.

Once you've been hired, the client expects you to produce accurate work at the scheduled deadline. Prioritizing everything will almost guarantee that you finish in time without forgetting something important.

As a virtual assistant, you're responsible for the upkeep of your business equipment. A client won't be responsible for providing you with all of the needed equipment to do your job. They expect you to be fully prepared to handle their challenging duties promptly.

CHAPTER 3

FINDING CLIENTS & GETTING HIRED

When you've created your work at home success plan, and you're ready to start recruiting clients and building your online business, it's time to put your brand message in front of thousands of potential clients.

One of the easiest ways to do this is with popular freelance marketplaces and community sites.

As a freelancer, you will want to become familiar with the most popular freelance marketplaces, because when you are just starting out, this is where you will generate a majority of your project orders as well as build a customer base so that you can secure ongoing work from regular clients.

While you can also build a large client base through direct marketing and advertising, by participating in the top freelance communities, you'll be able to maximize your exposure, and build a larger client base, in less time and quite often, with greater results.

You can also utilize freelance marketplaces to build credibility and establish yourself within the freelance community as a source of quality content or services.

The key to being successful within freelance marketplaces, isn't in bidding the lowest per project, or even on bidding on a great number of projects, in fact, if you are interested in making as much money per project as possible, you should never bid lower than you are comfortable with.

It's often too easy to undercut yourself by bidding low on projects in the attempt to secure work; after all, there are sometimes hundreds of other freelancers vying for the same projects.

But, if you really want to stand out and separate yourself from the low quality freelancers, keeping your pricing consistent and focusing only on projects that offer reasonable payment terms, you will quickly develop a reputation for quality - which will give your freelance business a tremendous boost, in terms of the type of clients you'll attract and the kind of money you can make.

Perhaps you want to take the work of other freelancers and manage them from the start. Using your own skills or a trusted partner you can simply polish "their" efforts, while you can create a business renowned for its quality and ability to add value.

If this sort of business sounds intriguing to you , here is a link http://www.thesimplesmartsystem.com it's a complete system that will show you step-by-step how to set a business like this up.

You'll also discover how to manage a business like this deftly, with very little work on your part, and how to profit quickly, as well.

Most importantly, it shows you how to find clients who are thirsty for the kinds of services you will provide.

I hope you enjoyed this free report and have taken away a "work- from-home" method that you will enjoy exploring.

CHAPTER 4

TIPS TO GETTING STARTED

Here are a few tips to help you get started as a professional freelancer:

TIP ONE: Offer More Value For Less

One of the best ways to stand out from your competition is to offer more value than your competitors. There are many ways to do this; it just takes a little creative thinking.

If you can't compete on price, then you have to go the extra mile and do things your competitors don't do.

Make your service look like it's 10 times better than that of your nearest competitors by offering additional value at no extra cost. These special incentives don't have to take up a lot of your time either. For example, offer the project in various formats, or offer to customize the document by including your clients name or website URL.

Here are a few ways to offer more value:

- Offer one free article for every 10 ordered.
- Offer HTML formatting for those who need it, at no extra charge.
- Offer PDF export at no additional charge.
- Offer to add images at no extra charge.
- Add formatting like table of contents for free with book writing.
- If you're a designer, include free graphics.

TIP TWO: Have a USP (Unique Selling Point)

Every business needs a unique selling point if they hope to be successful. Your unique selling point is something you offer that absolutely no one else offers.

Your USP should be something that really makes you stand out amongst your competitors. It should be either unique to you, if at all possible. This could be almost anything, but ideally it should be related to the market you're looking to work in.

Let's look at some examples of USPs for freelance writers:

- *College degrees*, especially in certain areas. For example, if you have a degree in nursing, this would be extremely helpful to people who need medical articles written!

- *Professional experience.* If you are a former veterinarian, you have a distinct advantage for someone who is looking to have pet care articles written.

- *Journalism experience.* If you have written for newspapers or magazines, this could set you apart. This would be especially helpful if, for example, you wrote full-time for a gardening magazine for ten years and someone was looking for gardening articles.

Bilingual. If you write fluently in more than one language, this could be a huge selling point! Many people need articles in other languages, but it can be very difficult to find someone who is fluent enough in both English and the other language to perform such a task.

- Affiliations. If you are affiliated with a certain group, you could have a very good advantage when it comes to writing articles for others in that group.

TIP THREE: Have Confidence In Yourself

When you're selling a service, you're not really selling what you DO; you're selling who you ARE.

The more confidence you have in yourself, the more others will believe in you. If you think you're the best, you'll be able to convince others you are, too!

TIP FOUR: Offer Phenomenal Service

Freelance writing is a service business, and the best way to get repeat business is to offer absolutely exceptional service.

There are many ways to be certain you're offering the best service possible.

- Offer a revision or two at no extra cost.
- Answer emails very promptly.
- Complete work AHEAD of schedule.
- If you think you can complete a job in two days, tell the client it will take four. When you finish it in two, he'll be thrilled!
- Offer volume discounts.
- Be extremely friendly.
- Be patient with excessive questions.
- Be polite, even when a client is rude.
- If you spot mistakes on your part, fix them BEFORE the client notices.

TIP FIVE: Communicate Regularly

One thing clients hate more than anything is being kept in the dark. When they've trusted their time, business, and money to someone, they want to feel assured that they've made the right decision.

When you keep in touch with a client, they'll know you haven't skipped town. They'll feel better that you're hard at work on their project and you aren't sunning yourself on the beach while they're waiting for their projects to be delivered.

If you're running behind schedule, don't be afraid to tell the client this. Do so BEFORE they ask, if possible. Most clients will understand, unless they have a very strict deadline. In this case, be prepared to offer a refund. Otherwise, as long as you stay in touch, most people will understand.

TIP SIX: Ask for Testimonials

Testimonials are a form of "social proof". When you have testimonials, you seem more trustworthy. This is especially true when you have testimonials from people who are well-known or highly-respected in the field you're working in.

If possible, get a picture and a URL you can include with each testimonial. This helps people believe your testimonials are real, especially when they can contact the person who gave it.

TIP SEVEN: Encourage Repeat Business

Repeat business is the lifeblood of almost any business. It costs a lot more to acquire a new customer than it does to retain an old one.

There are many things you can do to encourage people to keep returning to you for more work.

- Build a mailing list and send them regular mailings.
- Send your list special discount offers periodically.
- Offer special deals to regular clients.
- Give discounts for each milestone, such as 50, 100, and 200 pages ordered.
- Have a customer loyalty program, offering coupons or prizes to people who order regularly.
- Offer free work whenever you screw up. If you're late or make huge mistakes, give the client a major freebie.

TIP EIGHT: Offer Volume Discounts

It may seem counterintuitive to offer discounts when someone orders a lot from you. After all, it's more work, right? But these big orders might be where the bulk of your income comes from.

You need to offer these, so it's best to actually price yourself a bit higher than you really want to be paid. If the lowest you ever want to accept per page is $12, price yourself at $15 or $20. Then you can offer discounts to people who order a lot.

Start your discounts out at a relatively low number. The main thing you're looking to do is discourage people from ordering just one article at a time.

You'll have contact time spent with every client, but this is minimized if you can do several articles for the same client. It's much better to get larger orders than order for just one or two pages.

If your lowest price will be $12 per page, your scale might work like this:

- 1-4 articles are $20 each.

- 5-9 articles are $18 each.
- 10-19 articles are $16 each.
- 20-29 articles are $14 each.
- 30 or more articles are $12 each.

TIP NINE: Encourage Referrals

If you want to make more money, your business needs to grow. The best way to get it to grow is to have your current customers refer others. Some people will do this on their own, but many won't.

Some people will want to keep you all to themselves, fearing you'll become too busy to work for them when they need you. Others are just forgetful, or thoughtless, or even just rude. But many people will refer others if they're given an incentive to.

Incentives might include free articles, a percentage in cash (like an affiliate program), or other bonuses. You might give the client 1 page free for every 10 pages anyone they refer orders. This would not only encourage them to refer others, but also to refer those who might order in volume.

TIP TEN: Become Invaluable

The best way to make more money from your freelance writing is to become irreplaceable and absolutely invaluable to your clients. You need to make sure they keep coming back over and over by giving them exactly what they want at a price they can afford.

You should be consistently striving for the fastest turnaround time, the friendliest service, and the best prices you can possibly offer without selling yourself short.

You should NEVER under-price yourself severely. This will just burn you out and harm your business. Price your service reasonably, and fairly.

CHAPTER 5

FINDING ONLINE WORK

Here are the top methods of finding and securing high paying freelance opportunities:

Freelance Marketplaces

Make sure that any profiles you set up or samples of work that you send are exceptionally strong. Bid knowledgeably – research what a fair price for the work would be and bid near that.

www.elance.com – This site allows you to bid on a large variety of work, anything from article writing to copy. The writer is able to see a likely budget for the project, as well as how many other writers have placed a bid on the work.

After you have completed work, you will receive a rating.

Make sure that the work you submit for payment is of high quality, so your rating will remain high. The higher your rating and quality, the more likely you will receive higher payments for your work.

www.guru.com – This site is similar to Elance. Create a profile, search for work, place a bid and complete any bid that you are awarded. Be sure that any work you submit is of high quality.

www.getafreelancer.com – Do a thorough search on this site to sift through open projects that may fit your skills.

www.ifreelance.com – Check under "Provider Services" to create a profile and bid on projects.

www.scriptlance.com – Search carefully through this site for "writing" as many of the projects listed are programming related.

www.writingbids.com – On this site you can bid from anything ranging from books to resume writing; projects are taken from other bid sites and listed in this central location.

www.project4hire.com – Project for hire lists many different freelance projects, to bid you must register on their site.

www.totalfreelance.com – Total Freelance is another site where you can register to bid on freelance work.

www.writerlance.com – Register with Writer Lance to be able to bid on projects for freelance writers.

Here are other popular freelance opportunities available online:

www.associatedcontent.com – With Associated Content you post your own original work, and you receive a portion of money based upon how popular your article is and how much traffic you receive.

www.helium.com – Helium is similar to Associated Content, in that you post your own work and receive payment based upon how much traffic your article receives.

www.constantcontent.com – Using this site, you post your own original works and sell it outright for a set price.

www.suite101.com – With this site, you can post your own content and earn income on your writing based upon the popularity of your article.

When you apply for this work pay particular attention to responding as the employer specifies – you may need to submit a resume, portfolio, or samples of your work.

www.freelancewritinggigs.com – This site is a compilation of blogs, some of which post job leads.

http://jobs.problogger.net – A site geared towards job postings for Bloggers.

www.poewar.com – Navigate through to the freelance writing jobs, where you will find jobs compiled from many sources in one easy to view screen.

http://bloggerjobs.biz - Another site with a large listing of freelance blogging jobs.

www.mediabistro.com – Narrow your search on this job listing site by checking "freelance" to obtain only the listings that are freelance based.

http://jobs.freelanceswitch.com – This site includes a large listing of freelance writing job posting.

http://journalismjobs.com/ - Under "Opportunities", narrow your search down to just freelance writing jobs. There are plenty of opportunities on this site to view.

http://allfreelancewritingjobs.com – This blog provides weekly links to several job leads. You can also view previously posted jobs and apply to those as well.

http://www.wahm.com/jobs.html – This work at home forum lists many job openings; search through the listings to find those for freelance writers.

http://www.online-writing-jobs.com/ - This site also offers freelance writing job listings.

www.sologig.com – Under "Browse by Categories" select "creative", and you will find a few writing jobs, and many freelance copywriting jobs.

www.gofreelance.com – Go Freelance allows you to search by category – select "writing" and view listing for freelance writing.

www.freelancefree.com – A free site to register and find freelance work.

www.lancepost.com - Lancepost lists a feed of new job leads, sift through to find leads for freelance writing.